The Farm Animals

One sunny morning Jack went to see the French languasaurus who lived at the bottom of his garden. The languasaurus was delighted to see Jack, and they both said hello in French.

As Jack lived on a farm, the languasaurus had been wondering which animals there were on the farm. Jack wasn't sure, so they sent off an adventure to find out!

And the languasaurus decided it could be a good opportunity to teach Jack the French words for some farm animals.

The first animal they saw was a horse. The languasaurus told Jack that in French a horse was **un cheval**.

un cheval

Jack and the languasaurus said together **un cheval** as they clapped three times.

(And if you are reading this story now, join in too by saying **un cheval** as you clap three times.)

The next animal they saw was a cow. The languasaurus told Jack that in French a cow was **une vache**. So they said together **une vache** as they clapped twice.

(And if you are reading this story now, join in too by saying **une vache** as you clap twice.)

Jack knew their farm had recently got **des veaux** (some calves). The languasaurus wanted to know how many there were.

Let's count together **les veaux** (calves) in French:

un, deux, trois.

The next animal they saw was a pig. The languasaurus told Jack that in French a pig was **un cochon**.

Jack and the languasaurus said together **un cochon** as they clapped three times.

(And if you are reading this story now, join in too by saying **un cochon** as you clap three times.)

The languasaurus wanted to know how many pigs there were.

Let's count together **les cochons** in French:

un, deux, trois, quatre.

The next animal they saw was a duck. The languasaurus told Jack that in French a duck was **un canard**.

Jack and the languasaurus said together **un canard** as they clapped three times.

(And if you are reading this story now, join in too by saying **un canard** as you clap three times.)

The languasaurus wanted to know how many ducks there were.

Let's count together **les canards** in French:
un, deux, trois, quatre, cinq.

The next animal they saw was a sheep. The languasaurus told Jack that in French a sheep was **un mouton**.

Jack and the languasaurus said together **un mouton** as they clapped three times.

(And if you are reading this story now, join in too by saying **un mouton** as you clap three times.)

The languasaurus wanted to know how many sheep there were.

Let's count together **les moutons** in French:
un, deux, trois, quatre, cinq, six.

The next animal they saw was a hen. The languasaurus told Jack that in French a hen was **une poule,** so they said together **une poule** as they clapped twice.

(And if you are reading this story now, join in too by saying **une poule** as you clap twice.)

The farm now had **des poussins** (some chicks) and they looked so cute. The languasaurus wanted to know how many there were.

Let's count together **les poussins** (chicks) in French:

un, deux, trois, quatre, cinq, six, sept, huit, neuf, dix.

So on the farm there were ten chicks.

Jack now knew how to say in French all the different animals that there were on his lovely farm. Lets say them together:

It had been a fun morning, but Jack had to be back at the farm house for lunchtime. They had some family visiting this afternoon.

It was a nice sunny afternoon, so Jack and the languasaurus decided to go for a wonder around the farm. The languasaurus was keen to teach Jack how to say in French "**des légumes**".

Jack was rather puzzled at first. What could **des légumes** be?

But then Jack realised they were heading in the direction of the fields where all the vegetables were growing.

So **des légumes** were vegetables!

"Oh this is going to be fun!" thought Jack. He wasn't sure what they had growing on the farm this year, so it was going to be an interesting adventure!

"**Les carottes**" repeated Jack. Then he began to wonder what that could be. It sounded very much like carrots. But carrots were orange, and all he could see was green leaves!

The languasaurus starting digging. And out of the ground popped…

les carottes

The languasaurus had never tried **les carottes**, so Jack told him to try one.

So the languasaurus liked carrots!

That was good for Jack to know!

They then went into the next field.

Jack knew what these were! He loved popping open the pea pods and eating what's inside…..

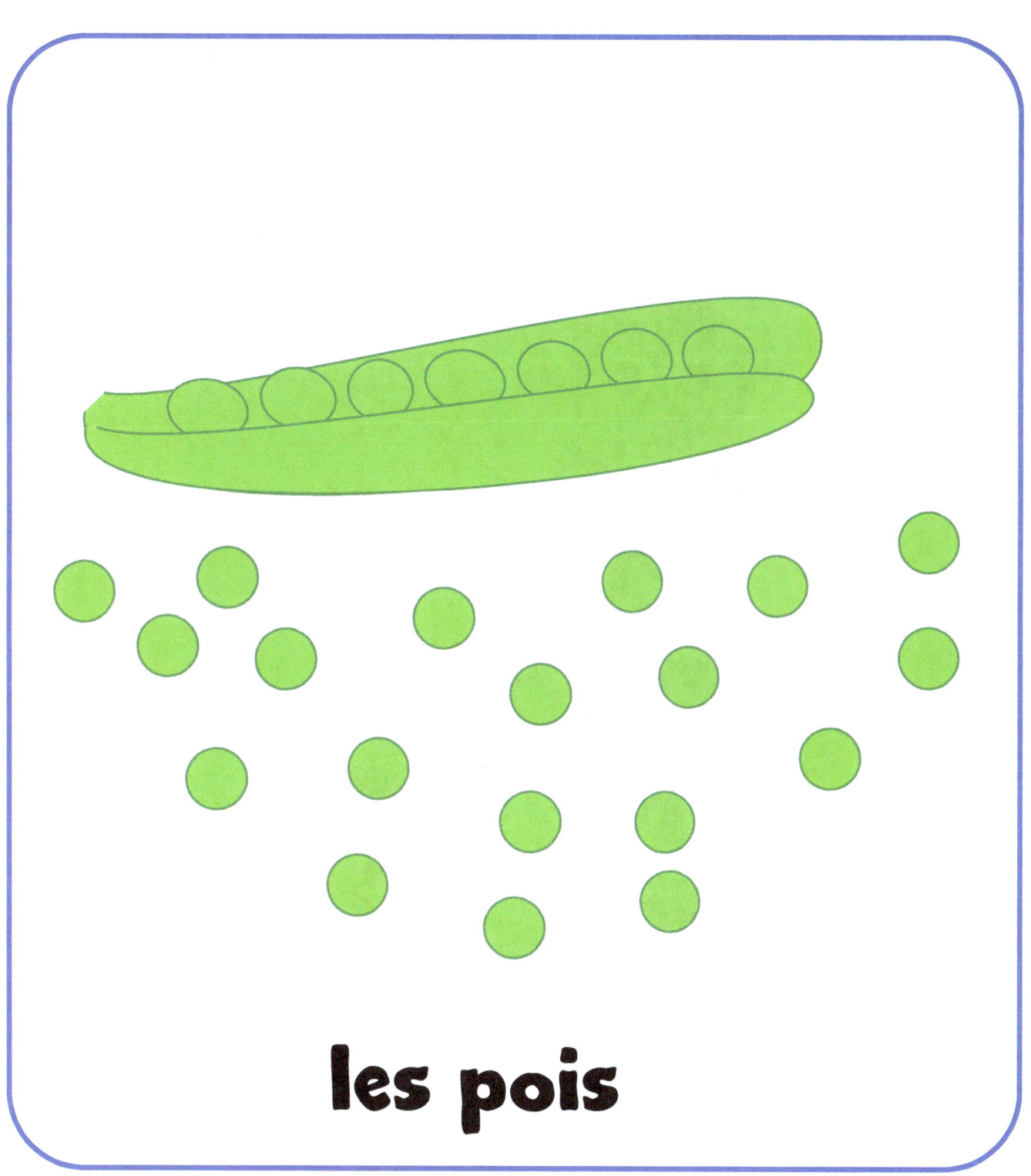

Les pois are peas in English!

Jack popped open a pea pod for his friend. He was curious to see if he liked them!

J'aime les pois.

Jack was pleased to hear that the languasaurus did like **les pois.**

The list of things he liked was getting longer!

In the next field, Jack wasn't really sure what they had growing:

What could **les pommes de terre** be? The languasaurus started digging and soon dug up….

les pommes de terre

Ah, so **les pommes de terre** is the French way of saying potatoes. The languasaurus had also not tried these. Would he like them?

The languasaurus said he didn't like potatoes!

"How strange!" thought Jack. Then Jack suddenly realised why. We always cook potatoes before we eat them. And the potato his friend had eaten, hadn't been cooked! Oops! No wonder he didn't like it!

Jack then noticed that his dad was in a nearby field. Jack was allowed to wonder about the farm, but they had been digging up vegetables and making a bit of a mess! So they hid in a nearby field were the plants were getting quite tall now!

Jack looked thoughtfully at the plants. What could **le mais** be?

Jack hoped the languasaurus wouldn't need to dig up another plant, as he didn't want to make any more mess!

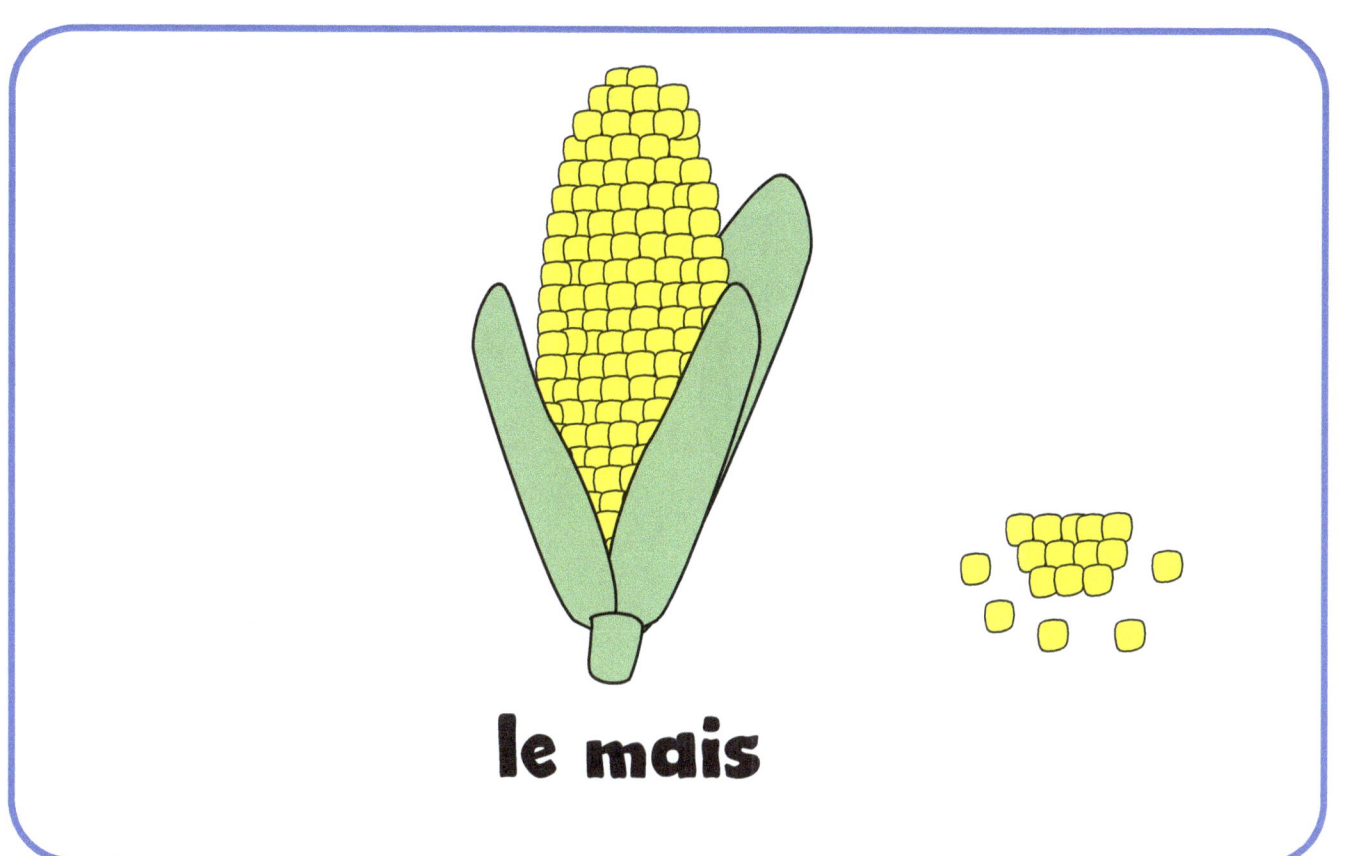

le maïs

Le maïs was sweetcorn! And luckily this just broke off the stem, so no digging and no mess!

J'aime le maïs.

Jack liked sweetcorn a lot, so he wasn't surprised to hear that the languasaurus liked sweetcorn too.

So there are lots of vegetables growing on the farm! Let's say together in French what vegetables there are!

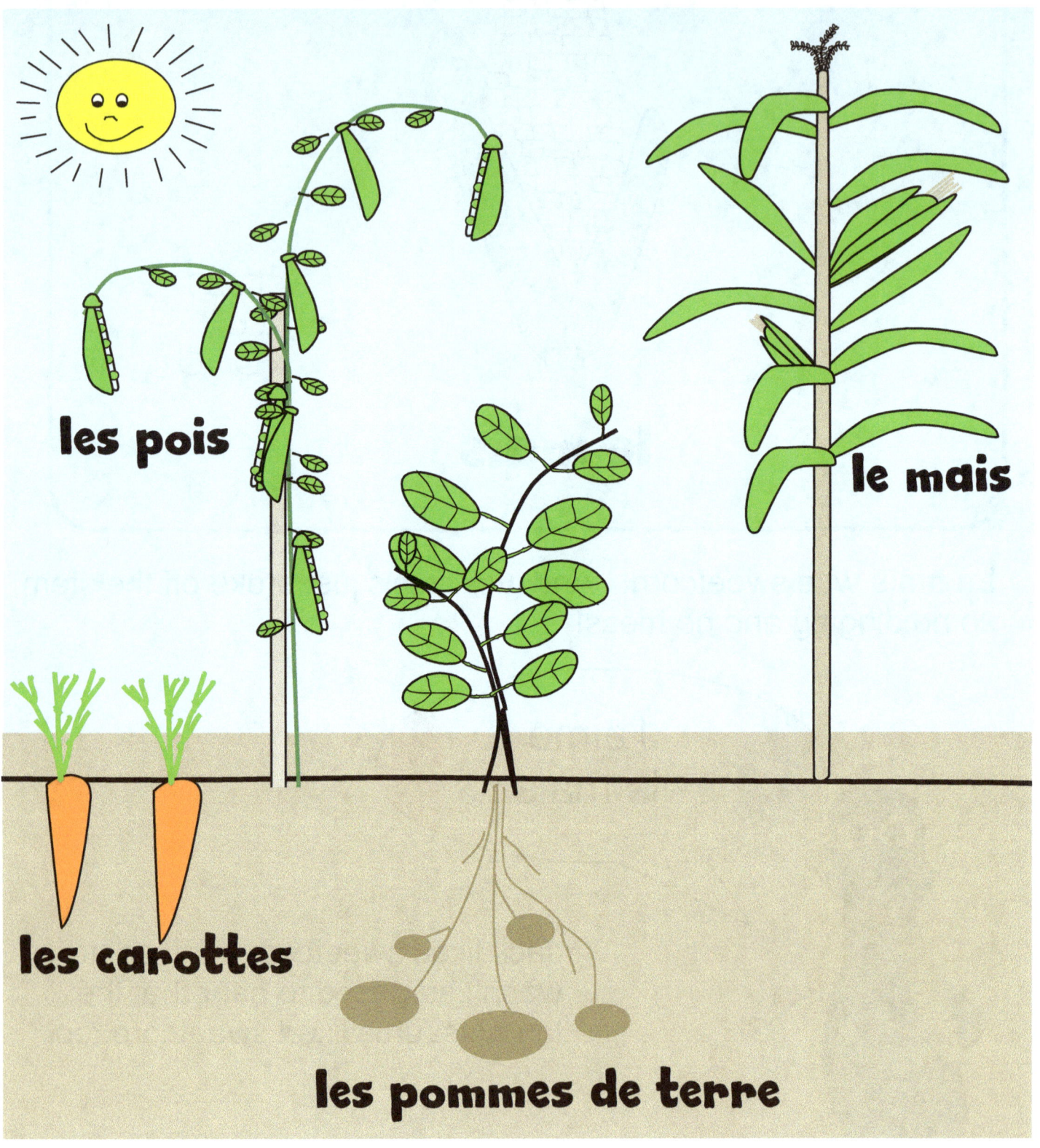

It had been so much fun discovering what was growing in the fields!

© Joanne Leyland   First edition 2018   Second edition 2021
This book may not be photocopied or reproduced digitally without the prior written agreement of the author.

Useful French words

un mouton
(a sheep)

un cochon
(a pig)

un cheval
(a horse)

un canard
(a duck)

une poule
(a hen)

un poussin
(a chick)

une vache
(a cow)

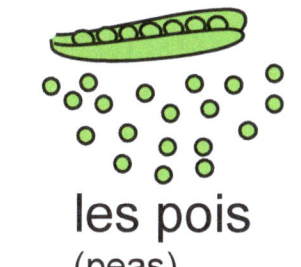
les pois
(peas)

le mais
(sweetcorn)

les carottes
(carrots)

les pommes de terre
(potatoes)

1	2	3	4	5	6	7	8	9	10
un	deux	trois	quatre	cinq	six	sept	huit	neuf	dix
(one)	(two)	(three)	(four)	(five)	(six)	(seven)	(eight)	(nine)	(ten)

© Joanne Leyland - This page may be photocopied by the purchasing individual or institution for use in class or at home

Let's sing a song!

The following words could either be sung to a made up tune, or you could try saying the words as a rap.

For inspiration of a melody to use you could hum first a nursery rhyme. How many different versions can you create using the lyrics?

À la ferme, À la ferme

Il y a, il y a

un cochon, un cochon

un mouton, un mouton

un cheval, un cheval

un canard, un canard

une poule, une poule

une vache, une vache

À la ferme - at the farm   il y a - there is / are

Follow on activity: Can you remember the correct order the animals appear in the story? Look back at the first story in this book to check if you are right!

© Joanne Leyland - This page may be photocopied by the purchasing individual or institution for use in class or at home

www.ingramcontent.com/pod-product-compliance
Lightning Source LLC
Chambersburg PA
CBHW081400080526
44588CB00016B/2552